The Making of a Champion

Inspirational Keys To Help
You Fulfill Your Destiny

by
Mike Murdock

Tulsa, Oklahoma

The Making of a Champion – Inspirational Keys
 To Help You Fulfill Your Destiny
ISBN 1-56292-091-X
Copyright © 1995 by Mike Murdock
P.O. Box 99
Dallas, Texas 75221

Published by Honor Books
P.O. Box 55388
Tulsa, Oklahoma 74155

Introduction

A champion — *Webster's New Collegiate Dictionary* defines a champion as "one who shows marked superiority." There are not many words that could describe being a champion better than that. It has been said that champions aren't born, they are made — one day at a time. And that is what this book is all about — making yourself into a champion.

After years of pursuing God's best for his life, Mike Murdock has discovered God's principles for being a champion. The quotes, keys and wisdom principles found on these pages will inspire and equip you to fulfill your destiny. You will learn to always reach for the best in life and not settle for less; to stand out from the crowd and not accept mediocrity. You will become a champion.

1

Winning doesn't start around you — it begins INSIDE you.

2

You can only conquer your past
by focusing on your future.

3

Your future begins with whatever
is in your hands today.

4

Stop looking at where you have been and start looking at where you are going.

5

Major on the opportunities,
not the obstacles.

6

Never justify failure.

7

You will never change
your life until you change
something you do daily.

8

Nothing will ever dominate your life
that doesn't happen daily.

9

The secret of your future is hidden
in your daily routine.

10

A successful life is often expensive.
It will cost you something to become
a champion. Time. Energy. Focus.

11

Success doesn't just "happen."
You set it in motion.

12

Champions seize their day.

13

Always remember the powerful importance of linking your habits to your life purpose.

14

Everything God creates is a
solution to something.

15

You are a life jacket to someone drowning.
Find them.

16

Your rewards in life are determined
by the problems you solve
for someone else.

≡ 17 ≡

The battle belongs to the persistent.

≡ 18 ≡

The victory will go to the one
who never quits.

16

≡ 19 ≡

Sometimes you have to do
something you dislike to create
something you desire.

≡ 20 ≡

Carefully review and fulfill any
vows, promises, or pledges you
have made to anyone.

≡ 21 ≡

Never promise what you cannot produce.

22

The quality of your
preparation determines the
quality of your performance.

23

Integrity is truthfulness. It is doing
what you say you will do.

24

Demand it from yourself
and reward it in others.

25

Your integrity will always
be remembered longer
than your product.

26

Utilize the strength of others.

27

Mentorship is the key to extraordinary success.

≡ 28 ≡

Someone is always observing
you who is capable of
greatly blessing you.

≡ 29 ≡

Those who unlock your compassion are
those to whom you have been assigned.

≡ 30 ≡

Go where your contribution is celebrated.

31

Two forces are vital to happiness:
your relationships and
your achievements.

32

You can be a marvelous influence for good.

33

Get involved in something great
and give your life to it.

34

Your success and happiness in life depends on your willingness to help someone solve their problem.

35

Failure is merely an opinion.

36

Nothing is ever as bad as it first appears.

Successful people are simply problem solvers.

≡ 38 ≡

Your entry can decide how you exit.

≡ 39 ≡

Your exit will be remembered
longer than your entry.

40

There are two forces that build that invisible gigantic machine called credibility that opens every door of success:

1) Trustworthiness
2) Expertise

41

You need your family.

42

You need a godly pastor.

43

Your mind gathers the dirt,
grime and dust of human
opinion every day. The Words
of God are like waterfalls...
washing and purifying your mind.

44

Get so excited over planning
your triumphs, you don't have time
to complain over past losses.

45

Happiness begins between your ears.

46

Someone has said, "Attitude determines altitude." Expect to conquer and master any obstacle you face today.

47

Overcomers know the inevitable
reward of reaching.

48

You are engineered for success.

49

You will never be promoted
until you become over-qualified
for your present position.

50

You will never correct what you
are unwilling to confront.

51

Never complain about what you permit.

52

Most people choose to sit as
spectators in the Grandstand of Life,
rather than risk the Arena
of Conflict to wear the
Crown of Victory.

53

Discover what motivates and excites you.

54

Pour yourself into something
you can believe in.

55

You will never reach
your potential until your
priorities become habitual.

56

Take time to do things right.

57

The weakness and flaws of any plan
are often buried by flurry and hurry.

≡ 58 ≡

One of the major causes
of failure is the unwillingness
to take the time to set your goals.

59

Stop asking yourself questions
that do not have answers.

60

Ask yourself creative questions such as,
"HOW can I improve the situation?"

61

Be ruthless with distractions.
Remember, creativity is the
search for alternatives.
Concentration is the
elimination of them.

62

Crisis always occurs at the curve of change.

63

Opposition gives birth to opportunity.

64

Every champion must be willing
to believe in his own dream
when others seem too busy or
uncaring to encourage him.

≡ 65 ≡

Those who created yesterday's pain do
not control tomorrow's potential.

≡ 66 ≡

Your success is on the other side
of scorn and false accusations.

67

Never expect a 16" x 20" idea to be celebrated by a 3" x 5" mind.

≡ 68 ≡

Evaluate your special gifts and abilities.

≡ 69 ≡

Pursue the career God equipped you for.

70

You will never have significant success with anything until it becomes an obsession with you.

71

Winners are simply ex-losers who got mad.

72

The proof of desire is pursuit.

73

As long as you can endure
a problem, you will not
reach for a remedy.

74

The first step toward success
is the willingness to listen.

75

Absorb the wisdom of great people.

76

Friends differ. Pinpoint those
who truly stimulate you...
educate you...placate you.

77

Do not build mental monsters
of fear and worry.

78

Expect others to respond
favorably toward you.

79

Set favor in motion for your
own life by planting seeds
in the lives of others.

≣ 80 ≣

Never share your troubles with
someone unqualified to help you.

≣ 81 ≣

Mentors are bridges to tomorrow.

82

You need problem-solvers in
your life. You need a good banker,
doctor and a financial advisor.

83

The way we talk, dress and act
reveals much about our character.

84

The atmosphere you permit
decides the attitude you convey.

≡ 85 ≡

Your words are continually
educating others around you.
Let them create a portrait
of enthusiasm and faith.

≣ 86 ≣

Avoid a complaining attitude.

≣ 87 ≣

Silence cannot be misquoted.

≡ 88 ≡

When you speak to others,
be concise. Be bold but
very distinct in what you say.
Do not leave room for
misunderstandings when possible.

≡ 89 ≡

Pay the price to stay in the presence
of extraordinary people.

≡ 90 ≡

Your best qualities will surface
in the presence of good people.

91

A winner never condescends,
but lifts those around him
to a higher mentality.

92

Refuse to bog yourself down
by placing blame on others.

93

Honesty is the hinge that swings open
the golden door of prosperity and success.

94

A winner never condescends,
but lifts those around him
to a higher mentality.

95

Your assignment is not your
decision but your discovery.

96

Accept work as God's gift,
not punishment.

97

Payday is simply reward day.
You are rewarded for spending
your energy and knowledge
in helping your boss or
company reach their goals.

98

Don't waste your life. It is too short,
valuable and irreplaceable.

99

Do not take today for granted.

100

Avoid time-wasters, such as bored
friends, unnecessary phone
calls and idle chatter.

101

Real champions complete things.
They are "follow through" people.

102

You will never possess what
you are unwilling to pursue.

103

Every task has an unpleasant
side...but you must focus on the
end results you are producing.

104

Life is a marathon, not a fifty-yard dash.

105

Patience is the weapon that forces
deception to reveal itself.

106

Whatever creates joy and energy within you is probably an indication of what God wants you to pursue.

107

Your greatest mistakes will happen
because of impatience.

108

Resist impatience.

≡109≡

Resist the temptation to accept
a job based on convenience
or pressure from friends.

≡ 110 ≡

Avoid sloppiness which
suggests a careless lifestyle.

≡ 111 ≡

Dress neat.

112

Invest in books, seminars, good clothing and other things that will increase your confidence and sense of worth.

≡ 113 ≡

The most powerful force
in the world today is the tongue.

≡ 114 ≡

Use your words to build confidence
in others. Refuse to slander another.

115

Boldly protect your ears and life from absorbing talk that does not edify and build.

≡ 116 ≡

Be bold in expressing your opinions.

≡ 117 ≡

Feel strongly about the things
that matter in life.

118

Listen to your own conscience.
It is a key to real success.

119

Don't poison your future
with the pain of the past.

120

Yesterday's failure can
become today's success.

121

Men do not really decide
their future...they decide
their habits — then, their habits
decide their future.

122

Refuse to be intimidated by
people or circumstances.

123

Adversity is breeding ground for miracles.

≡ 124 ≡

Those who do not respect
your time will not respect
your wisdom either.

125

Everything big starts little.

126

Successful people find daily
significance in 24 hours of progress.

127

None of us were born great.
You *became* what you are.
You discovered what you know.

128

Something is more important
than the packaging – the person.

129

You are a solution to somebody
with a problem.

130

When God created you, He gave
you certain gifts and talents
to accomplish something
He wanted you to do.

131

Make a "to-do" list each morning.

132

Great men simply have great habits.

133

Happiness is discovering ingredients that create a successful day...then, duplicating it regularly.

134

Preparation time is never wasted time.

135

A productive life is not an accident.

136

Find something that consumes you.
Something that is worthy of
building your entire life around.

137

Rejection is not fatal. It is merely someone's opinion.

138

You are already important.
You have nothing to prove to anyone.

139

Jesus never wasted time
with critics. He kept His attention
on His goal. He stayed focused.

140

Champions make decisions that
create the future they desire.

141

Planning cures disorder.

142

The Bible is God's blueprint for mankind. It defines His purpose for creating, as well as His covenant to bless us.

143

You cannot draw conclusions as long
as there is missing information.

144

Information breeds confidence.

145

Your strongest desires,
talents and opportunities
reveal God's calling and
dream for your life.

☰146☰

Never rewrite your theology
to accommodate a tragedy.

☰147☰

Your pain can become your passage
to the greatest miracle of your life.

148

Faith walks out,
when fatigue walks in.

≡149≡

Be a student of those who have
succeeded before you.

≡150≡

Appreciate the accomplishments of others.

151

Meticulously build your
foundation from friendship...
a support system that is the result
of thought instead of chance.

≡ 152 ≡

From the ashes of defeat burn
the greatest fires of accomplishment.

≡ 153 ≡

Your success depends on timing.

154

Every man fails. Champions simply get back up and begin again.

≡155≡

Time is money.

≡156≡

Treat it with the wisdom it deserves.

157

It is more productive to get ten men to work rather than you doing the work of ten men.

158

You are God's number one interest.

159

You were created for accomplishment.

≡160≡

You were not made to dig
in dirt with chickens, but
to soar the clouds with the
WINGS OF AN EAGLE!

161

You will never reach the palace
talking like a peasant.

162

Give some time and attention to your
own personal growth and development.

163

Knowledge is power.
The difference between failure
and success is information.

≡ 164 ≡

Everybody makes mistakes.

≡ 165 ≡

Failure is not fatal.

166

Every champion has discovered
that pain is seasonal. It will pass.
It is the passage to promotion.

≡ 167 ≡

Words are poison or power —
doubt or faith building.

≡ 168 ≡

Assess them accurately.

169

A popular, but inaccurate statement is, "words are cheap." Nothing could be farther from the truth.

170

You'll never leave where you are,
until you decide where you'd rather be.

171

Today is the tomorrow you
talked about yesterday.

172

Thousands will fail in life because they are unwilling to make changes.

173

What you love is a clue to
your calling and talent.

174

You will always remember what you teach.

≡ 175 ≡

As you assume the responsibilities
of the present, take time to enjoy
the privileges available to you now.

176

You are what you have decided to be.

177

Decisions create destinies.

178

Whatever brings you
the most fulfillment is
an important key to your life.

179

Only fools make permanent
decisions without knowledge.

180

Never assume your intuition
or perception is always correct.

181

Make decisions that will create the future you desire.

≡ 182 ≡

Always be where you are.

≡ 183 ≡

Life is a journey. Stay focused.

184

Do not permit your mind to race miles ahead of where your body is.

185

Those who are unwilling to lose, rarely do.

186

God made you to climb, not crawl.

187

Failure cannot happen in your life without your permission.

188

Losers discuss their obstacles.

189

Winners talk opportunities.

≡190≡

What you hear repeatedly, you will eventually believe.

191

What you make happen for others,
God will make happen for you.

192

Your words of kindness today could
easily create the wave that carries
someone to their dream.

=193=

Remind yourself throughout
today that each person you meet
has encountered waves of criticism,
condemnation and inferiority...
you can change this.

194

Money is what you receive when you help someone else achieve their goal.

195

Focus on all the little things that make life pleasurable.

≡196≡

You will only be remembered
for two things: the problems
you solve or the ones you create.

197

When you decide what you want,
the "How-To-Do-It" will emerge.

198

Information is the difference between
your present and your future.

199

Success is satisfying movement
toward worthwhile goals that
God has scheduled for your life.

≣200≣

Your mind is the drawing room
for tomorrow's circumstances.

≣201≣

Life is not a schedule of defeats,
but a parade of miracles.

202

You don't drown by falling
in the water, you drown
by staying there.

203

Everyone is a "well of information".
Draw from it.

204

Reward those who help you succeed.

⟆205⟆

Overcomers don't do it alone.
They conquer their pride.
They reject the trap of isolation.

≡206≡

God never consults your past
to determine your future.

≡207≡

Stop taking journeys into yesterday.

≡208≡

Always be where you are.
Taste NOW – it is the future
you have been talking
about your entire life.

209

Reject all feedback and comments
that breed doubt and defeat.

210

Those who do not increase you,
inevitably will decrease you.

≡ 211 ≡

Friendships are based
on mutual interests or mutual
problems. Be sure you know
the difference.

≡212≡

The only reason men fail is broken focus.

≡213≡

Champions talk faith because
their focus is on the finished results.

214

People laughed over the thought
of a horseless carriage.
Every extraordinary achiever
has been misjudged.

215

You are the creation of God,
made in His image.

216

Don't sell yourself short.
Don't belittle yourself.

217

It is not what men say about
you that really matters in life –
it is what you believe about yourself.

218

All men fall. The great ones get back up.

219

Champions simply make an extra attempt.

≡220≡

Champions do not become
champions in the ring.
They are merely recognized
in the ring. Their becoming,
happens in their daily routine.

221

Champions are rarely chosen
from the ranks of the unscarred.

222

Injustice is only as powerful
as your memory of it.

223

Recognize that adversity
has advantages. It will help you
decide what you really believe.

224

Make a daily appointment with God.

225

He who masters his time,
masters his life.

226

The evidence of God's
presence far outweighs
the proof of His absence.

227

Wisdom is the ability to interpret
a situation through God's eyes.

228

Unclutter your hour of prayer.
Miracles are at stake.

229

Though your failures are
planned by Hell, your recovery
is far more organized by Heaven.

Dr. Mike Murdock is in tremendous demand as one of the most dynamic speakers in America today. More than 11,600 audiences in 36 countries have attended his seminars and church auditorium crusades. He receives hundreds of invitations and travels over 150,000 miles each year to speak at colleges, schools, corporations and churches on the Laws of Success.

He is a well-known composer, and an accomplished pianist and singer. He has released more than ten albums to date and has had 57 books published.

He resides at his home in Dallas, Texas.

Dear Reader:

If you would like to share with us a couple of your favorite quotes or ideas on the subject of *the making of a champion* we'd love to hear from you. Our address is:

Honor Books
P.O. Box 55388, Dept. J.
Tulsa, Oklahoma 74155

Additional copies of *The Making of a Champion* and
other titles by Mike Murdock
are available at your local bookstore.

One-Minute Pocket Bible Series
One-Minute Devotional Series
Secrets for Winning at Work
Wisdom for Crisis Times
Seeds of Wisdom/Relationships

Tulsa, Oklahoma 74155